Disney

Miles FROM TOMORROWLAND

D1299043

ULTIMATE STICKER COLLECTION

How to use this book

Read the captions, then find the sticker that best fits the space.

Hint: check the sticker labels for clues!

There are lots of fantastic extra stickers for creating your own scenes throughout the book.

DK | Penguin Random House

Written and edited by Shari Last
Senior Designer Anna Formanek
Designers Anna Pond, Karan Chaudhary, and Pallavi Kapur
Pre-production Producer Kavita Varma
Producer Alex Bell
Managing Editor Sadie Smith
Design Manager Ron Stobbart
Publisher Julie Ferris
Art Director Lisa Lanzarini
Publishing Director Simon Beecroft

First American Edition, 2016
Published in the United States by DK Publishing
345 Hudson Street, New York, New York 10014

Page design copyright © 2016 Dorling Kindersley Limited
DK, a Division of Penguin Random House LLC
16 17 18 19 10 9 8 7 6 5 4 3 2 1
001–295423–Sep/2016

A catalog record for this book is available from the Library of Congress.

ISBN: 978-1-4654-5461-4

DK books are available at special discounts when purchased in bulk for sales promotions, premiums, fund-raising, or educational use. For details, contact: DK Publishing Special Markets, 345 Hudson Street, New York, New York 10014 SpecialSales@dk.com

Printed and bound in China

A WORLD OF IDEAS:
SEE ALL THERE IS TO KNOW
www.dk.com
www.disney.com

MILES

Miles Callisto is just like any other kid. He loves exploring, playing, and learning. There is one thing that makes Miles a little bit different: he lives in outer space! Let's meet him.

Space Boy

Miles wears a special spacesuit to keep him safe. His grav-boots stop him from floating away.

Messy

Miles cannot keep his bedroom clean, no matter how hard he tries!

HAPPY

Miles is almost always smiling. He loves outer space!

Best Friend

Miles's best friend is his robo-pet, Merc. Merc is a friendly robo-ostrich.

Space Mission

Miles and his family go on exciting missions in space. Miles can't wait for the next one!

Family Friends

Miles loves his family so much. They make a great team.

Best Job

Miles thinks he has the coolest job in the whole universe! Exploring space is so much fun.

To the Rescue!

If someone is in trouble, Miles can help. He is really good at solving problems.

OUTER SPACE

Outer space can be dangerous, but it is also amazing! Miles discovers so many [fasci]nating things during his space missions.

Planets

There are millions of planets in space. Which one will Miles travel to next?

Watson and Crick

This two-headed alien gives Miles and his family their space missions.

Atmosphere

[Huma]ns cannot breathe in space. [He] wears his helmet whenever [he lea]ves his spaceship.

TTA

The Callistos work for the Tomorrowland Transit Authority.

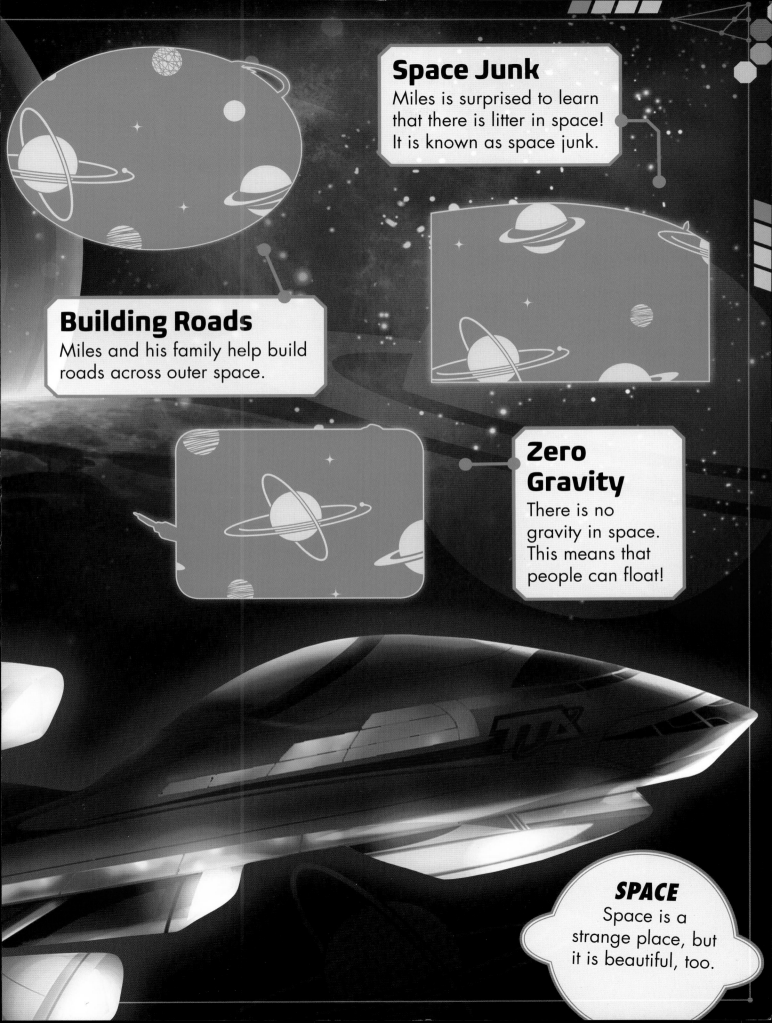

Space Junk
Miles is surprised to learn that there is litter in space! It is known as space junk.

Building Roads
Miles and his family help build roads across outer space.

Zero Gravity
There is no gravity in space. This means that people can float!

SPACE
Space is a strange place, but it is beautiful, too.

SPACE FAMILY

Miles Callisto and his big sister, Loretta, are very lucky. Mom is an ace space pilot. Dad is a genius inventor. The Callisto family lives and works in outer space!

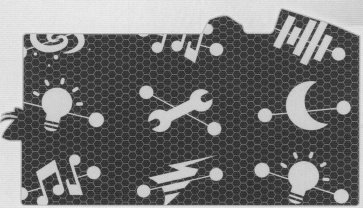

Captain Mom
Phoebe Callisto is a great mom. She is also one of the best pilots in the universe.

Smart Sister
Loretta Callisto is Miles's big sister. She loves learning all about space.

Dad the Inventor
Leo Callisto is an inventor. Miles wants to be just like him.

Family in Action
The Callisto family goes on lots of important space missions.

At Home
After an exciting mission, the Callistos relax on their spaceship.

Teamwork
The Callistos love working together. They always look out for each other.

Brave Uncle
Uncle Joe is a Captain in the SpaceGuard police force. He chases alien criminals!

AT WORK
The Callistos work hard because they love their job.

Use your extra stickers to create your own **BLASTASTIC** icy planet scene.

AWESOME GADGETS

With an inventor father, Miles and his family have some of the coolest gadgets in the universe! Which one is your favorite?

BlastBuckle
Miles uses his belt buckle to launch his BlastBoard.

QuestCom
The QuestCom is so useful. It can be a phone, a map, or even a flash beam.

BlastBoard
Miles loves his BlastBoard. It's like a flying skateboard!

Laserang
This laser boomerang is one of a kind. Miles has the only one!

MERC

Merc is a robo-ostrich. He is Miles's pet and best friend. Sometimes Merc gets into trouble, but he will do anything for Miles.

Rocket Boosters

Merc's wings can turn into super-fast rocket boosters. Zoom!

Telescopic Eyes

Merc's eyes can pop out and zoom in, like binoculars!

Robo Friends

Once, Merc made friends with a robo-dog and robo-cat.

Protective Pet

Merc is loyal to the Callisto family. He always wants to look after them.

Long Neck

Merc's neck can grow longer. This can be very useful!

Use your extra stickers to make your own cool **SPACESHIP** scene.

13

SPACE DANGERS

Space is dark, strange, and full of surprises. Miles and his family are always careful, but sometimes they find themselves in trouble—lots and lots of trouble!

Tiny Callistos

Oh no! Miles and his family have been shrunk by accident.

Captured!

Bad guy Gadfly has trapped Miles's family in a laser prison.

SURPRISE! In space, you never know what will happen next.

Engine Explosion

Kaboom! An engine has exploded. The Stellosphere needs somewhere safe to land.

Waterfall

Loretta is falling toward an icy waterfall. Help!

In the Dark

The Callistos are stuck on a planet with no electricity.

Space Snow

Evil Commander S'Leet has made it snow indoors! Can Miles save the day?

Dangerous Game

Miles must defeat a scary Dethalian alien in a game called Kalok.

Mystery Spaceship

Miles's Photon Flyer is being pulled into a spaceship. He must escape!

HOME IN SPACE

Miles and his family live on a spaceship called the Stellosphere. They enjoy family time while flying to their next space mission.

Stellosphere

The Stellosphere was built especially for Miles's family. It has everything they need.

Bio-Garden

There is a beautiful Bio-Garden on the Stellosphere. Fruit and vegetables grow there. Yum!

Bridge

The control center of the Stellosphere is called the Bridge.

Kitchen

The kitchen is where the family eats, talks, and throws pancakes in zero gravity!

Stella

The Stellosphere's computer is named Stella. She helps everything work properly.

Use your extra stickers to create your own **SUPERSTELLAR** space scene.

VEHICLES

Each space mission needs a different vehicle. Will Miles need a small, speedy spaceship or a strong robotic suit? Which vehicle would you choose?

Scout Rover

The scout rover has enormous tires for driving on rocky, bumpy planets.

Photon Flyer

Miles built his own super-fast ship. It has a seat for Miles and another for Merc.

Captain Miles

Miles loves to speed through space in his Photon Flyer!

Exo-Flex

This robotic suit is strong enough to smash through walls. Boom!

Merc

Miles sometimes uses Merc as a vehicle. The robo-ostrich is a comfortable ride.

Skis

When there is deep snow, sometimes skis are better than any vehicle.

StarJetter

This small spaceship is perfect for a short visit to a planet.

HANGAR

The Stellosphere has its own hangar. All the smaller vehicles are kept there.

NO PROBLEM!

Miles and his family make a great team. They are really good at working together on their missions. They are learning to use their skills to solve tricky problems.

New Inventions

Leo is always thinking of new inventions. He hopes they will be useful during a mission.

High Five!

It's awesome when Miles and Loretta save the day together.

Family Meeting

Sometimes, Miles's parents call a family meeting. Everyone can think of ideas together.

Big Plans

It is important to make careful plans before going on a dangerous mission.

Trust

Miles trusts his family completely. Even if he is scared, Miles knows he will be safe.

Computer Skills

Loretta is REALLY good at computers! This helps solve lots and lots of problems.

Crazy Ideas

Once, Merc used his boosters to defrost a frozen object. It was a crazy idea, but it worked!

HELP IS HERE

Solving problems is an important part of every mission.

MILES'S FRIENDS

Miles has lots of friends. Some are humans and some are aliens! Miles has so much fun when he goes on an adventure with his friends.

Prince Rygan
Rygan is a friendly alien prince. He helps Miles escape from prison.

Pipp Whipley
Pipp lives underwater! He is really good at fixing things.

Mirandos
Mirandos is a computer expert and a great friend.

Blodger Blopp
This smiley, blobby alien is one of Miles's best friends.

Haruna Kitumba
Haruna is Miles's friend from back on Earth. Now they both live in space.

THE BAD GUYS

Space is not just full of space dust and space junk. There are some bad guys out there, too. What do these bad guys want? Miles will find out and try to stop them!

Dibblex

Do you have anything shiny? Dibblex wants to take it! This thief loves sparkly things.

Gadfly Garnett

The most wanted villain in all of space! Gadfly is as sneaky as an alien can be.

Holo-Goon

Gadfly can create a Holo-Goon soldier to help him cause trouble.

Queen Gemma

Gemma is an alien queen. She thinks that Miles and his family want to make trouble.

Blizzbert and Flurrbo
These little ice aliens work for scary Commander S'Leet. They are clumsy and funny.

Commander S'Leet
Commander S'Leet is an evil ice alien. He wants his own planet to rule over. Beware!

FUZZIES
Dibblex has an army of fluffy little thieves called Fuzzies.

ALIEN OUTLAW

Gadfly Garnett is one of the most wanted villains in space. He is always working on an evil plan—and always running away from the SpaceGuard police!

Wanted Criminal

Captain Joe is looking for Gadfly Garnett. Has anyone seen him?

Stop, Thief!

Gadfly steals a powerful rift drive. He doesn't realize Miles is watching.

BAD GUY

When Gadfly appears, everyone knows there is going to be trouble.

Floating Villain

Not even Gadfly Garnett can escape zero gravity!

Wrong Captain

Once, Gadfly tried to steal the Stellosphere! Luckily, Miles stopped him.

Goon Army

Gadfly uses the yellow rings around his wrists to create a Holo-Goon army.

Surprise!

Gadfly once saved Miles when he fell down a cliff. Miles was very surprised.

Under Arrest

Caught again! Will sneaky Gadfly try to escape again?

SPACE ALIENS

Miles meets many aliens on his space adventures. Some are friendly while others are scary. They are always strange!

Quarkons

These colorful Quarkons love music and singing.

Mr. Xylon

Miles's postman is an alien with four arms. His name is Mr. Xylon.

Fuzzy Rock

Miles once found a fuzzy rock. It kept growing bigger and bigger!

Scorabs

These scary alien bugs live in the shade. They don't like the light.

Rock Aliens

These rocks are alive! Miles gives them a ride on his BlastBoard.

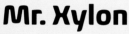

Use your extra stickers to create an amazing **ALIEN PLANET** scene.

AMAZING ADVENTURES

Miles loves his job. Every day is a new mission, which means that every day is a new adventure. What is going to happen tomorrow?

Spacewalk
Hold on tight! Miles, Blodger, and Merc go for a spacewalk.

Joining the SpaceGuard
Uncle Joe takes Miles and Merc on a SpaceGuard police mission.

Riding on Quarkons
Miles and Loretta take a ride on these cool space creatures.

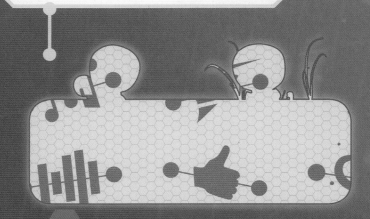

Alien Dinosaurs!
Once, a space dinosaur chased Miles across a planet. Luckily, Miles was faster!

Kalok

Miles climbs to the top of a floating wall to win a game of Kalok.

Planet in Danger

Sometimes missions are full of danger, especially when Commander S'Leet's about.

New Mission

What is the next mission? Admirals Watson and Crick are ready to tell us.

ZOOM!

There's nothing better than flying through space!

CRAZY PLANETS

There are millions of planets in space. Some are hot, some are cold. Some are beautiful and some are dangerous. Miles hasn't been to all of them yet, but he wants to try!

Plant People
Miles and his family had a surprise on this planet. The plants can talk!

Cold as Ice
This planet is covered in ice mountains and freezing rivers.

Pretty Planet
Miles and Merc have never seen a planet as pretty as this one.

Crystals
Wow! Look at all the glittering crystals that cover this planet!

Caves
One planet had a maze of dark caves. Miles almost got lost!

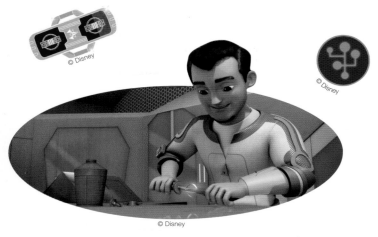

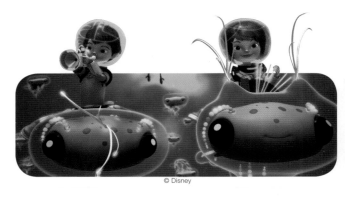

Riding on Quarkons

Dad the Inventor

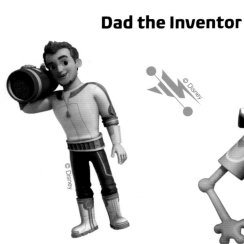

New Inventions

Mr. Xylon

Caves

Under Arrest

QuestCom

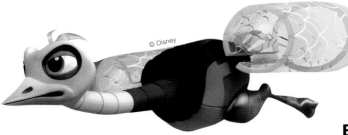

Rocket Boosters

Goon Army

Joining the SpaceGuard

Loretta

Wrong Captain

Laserang

Gadfly
Flies

Pretty Planet

Telescopic Eyes

Crystals

Thinking

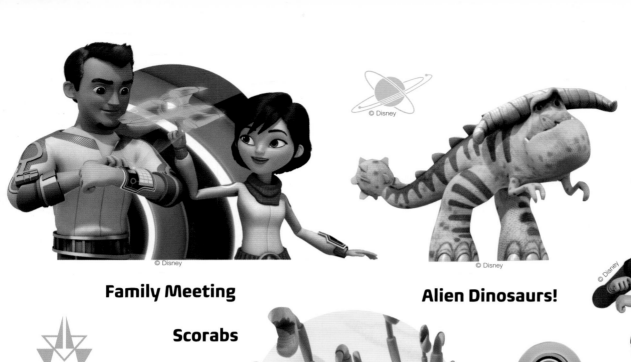

Family Meeting

Alien Dinosaurs!

Scorabs

Brave Uncle

Miles's Mom

Stop, Thief!

Planet in Danger

High Five!

Family in Action

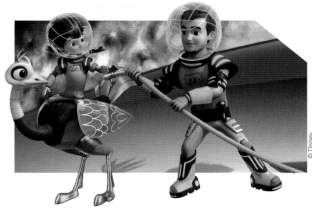

Trust

Robo Friends

Kalok

BlastBoard

Goon Trap

Speedy Ostrich

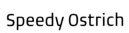

Rock Aliens

Floating Villain

Plant People

Super-fast

Computer Skills

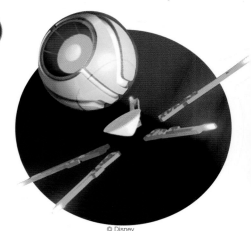

IOTA

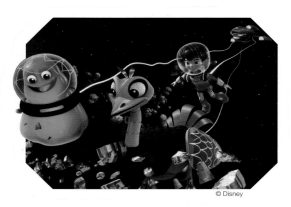

Space
Speeder

Fuzzy Rock

Spacewalk

Captain Mom

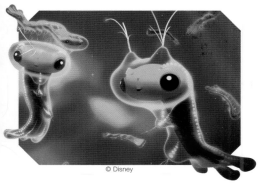

Quarkons

Long Neck

BlastBuckle

Wanted Criminal

Smart Sister

Crazy Ideas

New Mission

Cold as Ice

Eyescreen

Teamwork

Big Plans

BraceLex

Protective Pet

Trouble

Surprise!

At Home

To the Rescue!

Blizzbert and Flurrbo

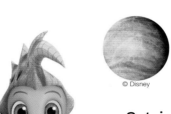

Ostrich Pal

In the Dark

Prince Rygan

Waterfall

Space Junk

Stellosphere

StarJetter

Space Boy

Skis

Zoom!

Queen Gemma

Building Roads

Captured!

Kitchen

Bio-Garden

Family Friends

Mirandos

Watson and Crick

Dethalian
Alien

Commander S'Leet

Dad's Lab

Engine Explosion

Flying Fast

Queen and Prince

Zero Gravity

Merc

Photon Flyer

Space Mission

Dibblex

Pipp Whipley

Best Job

Haruna Kitumba

Mom and Miles

Bridge

Gadfly Garnett

Space Snow

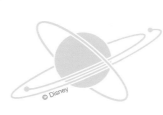

Scout Rover

Planets

Messy

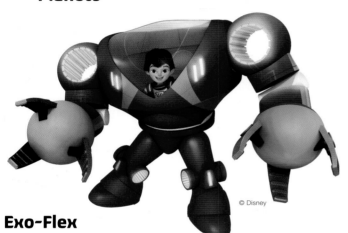

Exo-Flex

Blodger Blopp

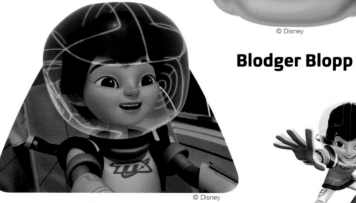

Stella

Captain Miles

Blast Off!

Tiny Callistos

Dibblex Captured

No Atmosphere

Dangerous Game

Best Friend

TTA

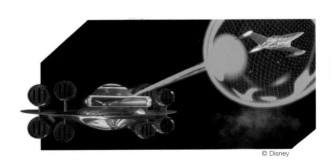

Mystery Spaceship

Holo-Goon

EXTRA STICKERS

EXTRA STICKERS

Extra Stickers

Extra Stickers

© Disney

Extra Stickers

Extra Stickers

Extra Stickers

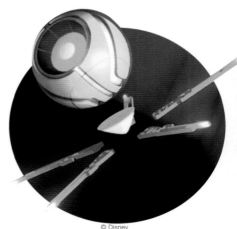

Extra Stickers

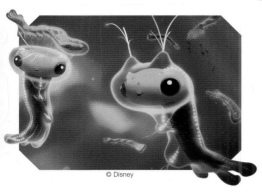

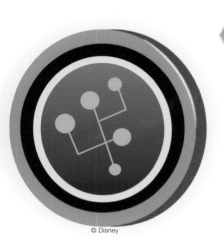

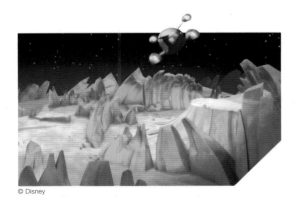

Extra Stickers

© Disney

© Disney

© Disney

© Disney

© Disney

© Disney

© Disney

© Disney

© Disney

© Disney

© Disney

© Disney

© Disney

© Disney

© Disney

© Disney

© Disney

© Disney

© Disney

Extra Stickers

Extra Stickers

Extra Stickers

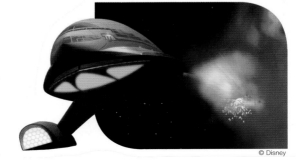

© Disney

Extra Stickers

Extra Stickers

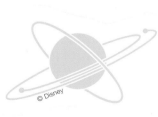

Extra Stickers

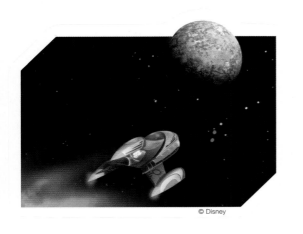

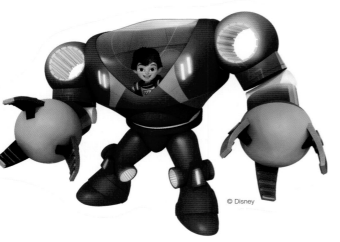

Extra Stickers

© Disney

© Disney

© Disney

© Disney

© Disney

© Disney

© Disney

© Disney

© Disney

© Disney

© Disney

© Disney

© Disney

© Disney

© Disney

© Disney

EXTRA STICKERS

EXTRA STICKERS